M000224018

He Kept Me…Through the Laundry

Gladys Evans Peoples, PhD

He Kept Me…Through the Laundry

Entegrity Choice Publishing
PO Box 453
Powder Springs, GA 30127

The views expressed in this work are solely those of the author and do not necessarily reflect the views of the publisher, and the publisher hereby disclaims any responsibility for them.

Unless otherwise indicated, Scripture quotations used in this book are from the Holy Bible, New International Version (NIV).

Book Cover Designed by
Kylie Dayton
kyliehd@comcast.net

ISBN: 978-0-9909397-0-2 (sc)
ISBN: 978-0-9909397-1-9 (hc)
ISBN: 978-0-9909397-2-6 (e)

Library of Congress Control Number: 2015931263

Printed in the United States of America

Dedication

I dedicate this book to my four laundry collecting gifts from God: Tayt, Titus, Bayli and Madyson. God used your individual habits and collective laundry practices to not only cultivate my spiritual growth, but also reveal secrets about His people and their continuous need for divine cleansing. I pray that you will use this book as a springboard to help you understand the necessity of actively pursuing the voice of God in every area of your life. If you are quiet, trust God and expectantly listen, you can hear Him can speak through anything-even your dirty laundry.

It is my deepest desire that you tirelessly seek to gain a clean heart, gratefully welcome God's cleansing methods and intentionally follow His directions so that you may march into your destiny lacking nothing. I am grateful for and love each of you.

Acknowledgements

With utmost reverence, I thank my God for selecting me to pen this message to help His people. I am truthfully in awe of the way in which the Holy Spirit poured this book into me and I exalt my Savior and Lord, Jesus the Christ for making all things possible. Jesus is love and with more than I can say, I love and give Him total praise. All the glory forever belongs to God!

My gratitude is extended beyond words to my sister, Patti for her reassurance on drought days and vision for the impact of this little, big book. I thank God for the gift of you.

Special thanks to my brothers, Jimmy and Shawn. I am grateful for your relentless push and commitment to seeing this work published and into the hands of hurt people.

To my remaining siblings, devoted friend Tammy, MaRita and Roxie, I appreciate your prayers and encouragement. Thank you from my heart.

I also wish to acknowledge my dear friend, Bobbie. Your honest feedback and willingness to focus on this work during your most difficult time has helped redefine my definition of friendship. Our lives are intertwined for a greater divine purpose.

Contents

Introduction

This book is not solely about gathering, sorting and washing dirty clothes. It will not provide you with an outline on how to clean your garments most efficiently, list paramount cleaning supplies or even propose suggestions for saving money during the laundering process. It will not recommend the most water efficient washing machines or energy preserving dryers to purchase.

Instead this book is an inspired revelation that provides a glimpse into the multifaceted lives of women and the methods by which they can become righteous daughters of God. It compares the assorted collection of dirty laundry to the complex character traits of individuals and parallels the simple cleaning process of the washing machine to the means God uses to cleanse the hearts of His children.

Much like the process required for adequately cleaning laundry, women acquire sin stains that must be washed by God to optimize use of their lives. Accordingly, this book relates the repetitive laundry assemblage to five dispositions commonly displayed by women as they navigate through their life journey responding to and or hiding from their experiences and core belief system. Within these personality types, numerous women regularly trade one messy situation for another and fail to realize that God is relentlessly pursuing them to dispose of their muck. Some women maintain a complex disguise, role play through life and secretly doubt

God's willingness to help them advance to the next level. While in contrast; others are stuck in their current state waiting on God or someone else to miraculously create a better life for them. Additional personas result in women repeating independent quests to improve the problematic regions in their lives far away from God's changing power or abandoning their foundational beliefs and acquiring unmoral character traits as they ascend in their profession. This book uses the process of washing dirty clothes to help women identify the areas of their life that need to be washed and show them the systematic approach God uses to make them clean.

The Laundry Struggle

Shortly after my divorce was legally finalized, I began to struggle with managing the enormous amount of perpetually accumulating dirty laundry. I thought I would lose my mind trying to keep enough clean clothes for my children to wear without clear evidence of filth and unpleasant aromas marching succinctly behind their every step. In addition to their clothing, I had mounds of other household items awaiting my undivided attention. It seemed as though the very instant I folded and put away the last clean item; every laundry basket in the house was overflowing again.

Initially, I was unsure why the laundry had become so significant because I had always gathered and completed all of the washing. With one less person in the house, there certainly were fewer items to be cleaned. However, if one of my children inquired about any garment, I would reply with a dissertation about how hard I worked, how unappreciated I was and how I could not do all this labor by myself. It is somewhat comical now, especially since the requested item was usually only a favorite pair of jeans, a sock mate or an Aeropostale t-shirt. My children must have known I was extremely frazzled because after a while, they stopped asking me questions about anything associated with the laundry.

I cried about the laundry, fussed about the laundry, told everyone who would listen about my excessive laundry and then finally prayed about the laundry. Regrettably, my negative fixation on the dirty clothes accrual was altering my usual disposition and interfering with my relationships with my children. I had to find an alternative for the whining and complaining, so I sought God.

While floundering, I thankfully retained enough wisdom to know that God was concerned about my daily struggles. I recalled Peter's declaration to cast all my anxiety on God, for He cares for me (1 Peter 5:7). I believed that although God wanted me to do the things I could for myself; He would listen to my concerns and accompany me through the difficulties. For that reason, I prayed not for the laundry to cease or for someone else to do it, but that the laundry would become a less significant burden for me.

After almost six months of praying and learning not to stress or complain about my repetitive responsibility (I know, that's a long time), I concluded that laundry was like breathing, both automatically happen. I accepted the reality that we do not even have to think about the breathing process; the fact that we are alive lets everyone know that we are breathing at some rate.

Laundry is no different than this recurrent involuntary breathing practice. Laundry accumulates as individuals physically exert themselves, maintain a basic level of cleanliness or participate in their daily routines. While concentrated conscious efforts can decrease the amount of laundry, even the most perfected methods will not eliminate dirty clothes altogether. Regardless of the environment, family routines or efforts, laundry, like breathing, just happens!

The Revelation

One day while performing my humdrum laundry duties, the Spirit of the Living God revealed to me that the actual laundering process was parallel to the techniques He uses to cleanse His people and prepare them to move into their ordained destiny. It is crucial to note that I only heard the Holy Spirit when I ceased complaining, decided to thank God that I had a washer and dryer in my home (this wasn't always the case), accepted the constant buildup and was determined to simply complete the task before me. He may have been trying to reveal this long beforehand, but my "woe is me" attitude and negative tongue likely kept me from hearing anything from God.

Hence, I beg you to approach unpleasant responsibilities in quietness and with an expectation that God will expose what you need to learn from the experience. As a former supervisor of mine frequently declared, "Fake it, 'til you make it." Candidly stated, "Close your mouth and do not complain or even discuss your many responsibilities." Instead of concentrating on the reality, act like you know it is a privilege to complete the tasks before you. It is momentarily unimportant how you truly feel about the undertakings. You must deliberately focus on the positive aspects of the work to gain the reward. All the "act likes" will become a reality as you will no longer have to pretend; but you will become genuinely grateful throughout the tasks at hand which opens the gateway for you to hear from God.

This concept is crucial for women to begin the change process. Although we are busy with gender responsibilities and are fixers by nature, women must positively approach all their overloads with gratefulness to hear the voice of God as the first phase in being washed clean. Paul reminds us to, "Let our gentleness be evident to all. The Lord is near. Do not be anxious about anything, but in every situation, by prayer and petition, with thanksgiving, present our requests to God. And the peace of God, which transcends all understanding, will guard our hearts and our minds in Christ Jesus" (Philippians 4:5-7).

We must come to accept that despite our negative or

occasional hostile feelings toward our unpleasant duties, in this progression of life there will always be some type of work to complete that necessitates a chosen positive approach. Rather it is physical labor required to maintain a clean environment or growth needed in our personal lives, we should embrace the undesirable moments and challenging obstacles as opportunities for development. This upgrade of both our physical and spiritual surroundings will, at the very basic level, require purging with water and cleaning agents for constructive change. While certain marks will be washed away quickly, some of our longstanding habits, grime and sin stains will require extra work and specialized formulas to be removed. Left untreated our garments and lives will become dull, faded or inadequate for their intended purpose.

Throughout the next pages of this short book, it is my goal to encourage you to transform your attitude toward unwelcomed responsibilities through an examination of dirty laundry. As you read through the brief description of my own laundry collectors' habits, you will obtain a fresh understanding of your own assortment of laundry. You will gain insight far beyond the massive buildup of dirty clothing to an unfathomable discernment of what dirty laundry truly represents in your life. Even more, as you begin to analyze the behaviors in your home, what you once solely viewed as filthy dry goods, scattered fabrics and a repetitive annoyance will become the hinge that swings the gate open toward your path of interior cleanliness and peace.

You will recognize your need for continuous development. You will allow God to escort you through the repetitive cycles and soakings to clean, purify and make you ready to walk in His righteousness throughout all expanses of your life. My sincerest longing for you is that you will begin to identify parts of your life that need to be changed, open your heart to receive God's cleansing power and accept His methods as the only way to gain freedom from the mire that keeps you from moving forward into your destiny. My own willingness to be cleansed and acceptance of God's procedures kept me calm, protected, stable and grateful through my laundry. I trust that God will provide you with the same contentment through your own dirty laundry.

ONE

The Overflow

So we fix our eyes not on what is seen, but on what is unseen.
For what is seen is temporary, but what is unseen is eternal.
2 Corinthians 4:18 (NIV)

Have you ever asked yourself, "How in the world do I have so much laundry?" or perhaps like me, you have asked, "How in the world do these people dirty so many clothes?" If you have children who are old enough to independently change their clothes, a spouse with poor laundry habits or a borderline obsession for fresh clothing or perhaps you have a fervent longing to have your laundry basket vacant at all times; you are acquainted with the challenge to finish the laundry. It simply does not get finished. The moment you exhale a sigh of relief that this task is completed, checked off the list and over until next week; you discover at least one important item that did not make it into the washing machine. It is at this very instant that you say to yourself, with a groan of frustration, "Here I go again." Most women or the "Laundry Doers" (I believe this to be a significant title deserving capitalization) in the house are familiar with this unfailing dilemma—the overflow of dirty clothes.

Others in the house cannot grasp the magnitude of this continuous accumulation or comprehend why we spend so much time repeating the same activity. They cannot understand our elevated voices when, in the middle of doing the laundry, we discover the pants are inside out, clothes are left on the floor behind the bathroom door and the newly purchased pair of socks does not have its mate. Even more, they cannot fathom why we insist that the current cycle of laundry be attacked before we participate in fun activities or why we simply do not ignore the laundry all together and enjoy the weekend. When all is said and done, they do not have a clue why we, the Laundry Doers, believe that laundry is such a big deal.

This lack of understanding most often stems from the family's limited knowledge of how quickly the laundry expands and their failure to actively participate in the never ending duty that must be upheld to function within acceptable parameters of cleanliness. Furthermore, the annoyed family members momentarily forget that they will soon ask the Laundry Doers to locate the items they cannot or why certain articles have not yet been cleaned.

As the overseer of all clothing and mother of four school-aged children, I completely understand this madness as I have an enormous amount of laundry collected weekly in my home. Although clothes are usually washed daily, there is ALWAYS something left in the laundry basket, bed linens to be refreshed or random murky items scattered throughout the house that have not made their way to the laundry room.

This scenario begs the question, what is overflowing in your life? What are the lingering situations that you can never seem to completely wrap your arms around or complete? These are the surplus issues that others do not understand or even attempt to comprehend. They keep you perplexed, frustrated and stuck. These troubling matters are the very conditions that God desires to cleanse and remove from your life to propel you forward.

Two-Load Method

Because I am a single parent with a high-pressure, full-time job and multiple laundry collectors; I have finally resolved (by the grace of God) that I will no longer be a perfectionist with the upkeep of clean clothes. I simply view laundry as something that has to be done. I do not obsess over dirty articles of clothing in the wash basket or on the floor. I do not spend my days thinking about my need to wash, fold and put away clothing in their proper place. In fact, I believe I have now become a bit lackadaisical about the entire laundry process. If the clothes are dark, they go in one load; if the clothes are white or light, they go in the other load. The clothes lingering outside the black/white spectrum are flexible. Depending on how early in the morning or late at night I am washing clothes and the immediate need for usage the, "I'm not white or black items" may be joined to either load.

The serious Laundry Doer has likely concluded that I am at least two standard deviations below laidback and convinced that I need to surrender this task to someone else. Other readers, especially those with three or more children probably recognize my hurried system and believe it makes good sense. That or they are annoyed at themselves for having been so meticulous about the whole process and not using my less tedious method.

Nevertheless, amazingly my strategy for doing laundry has only produced a few items with a new hue. My children have never complained about their clothes or at least not enough to encourage me to change my technique. I am not certain if this attitude of gratefulness is because at least two of them are old enough to wash their own clothes or if their unvoiced displeasure is due to sheer satisfaction and appreciation of my doing their work for them. As a mother who consciously strives to be a parent with whom God is pleased, I prefer to believe the latter. Whatever the actual reason though, my system for attacking the laundry works in my home.

Do you have a strategic approach for managing your overloads? Are your methods dated and in need of alteration to obtain greater success? Or are you ignoring the needed adjustments for your issues and silently suffering because no one else is complaining? Have you settled in your current state? God longs to assist you with managing and reducing your concealed loads; however, you must be willing to ask Him and receive His methods.

Chunk It

On a larger scale, I liken cleaning dirty laundry to every other major task in our lives. I believe there should be some specific method or strategic plan to accomplish both our short and long term goals. That plan may be as simplistic as my two-load method or contain intricate details that cause the most scholarly minds to be momentarily perplexed. Whatever the system of attack, I maintain that we usually need to chunk our tasks and complete our jobs in sections. If we try to complete major goals all at once or in a rushed period of time, we frequently become overwhelmed by the magnitude of the objective and quit long before we make noticeable progress. However, a steady focus on the anticipated results, while working on one load at a time, will almost certainly yield steady growth toward the preferred conclusion. To that end, there must be a plan for every endeavor. If there is no design, we become frustrated with the task and avoid the duty altogether or we dash through the chore half-heartedly merely to say we have completed our job.

Laundry is no different. I have learned from experience that ignoring the laundry or skirting through it does not harvest pleasant results. Mold can grow outside a science laboratory, required undergarments do run out and wool sweaters will shrink when submerged in water. I am absolutely certain that failure to commit intimate time to this task will result in an overwhelming expansion of clothes, unpleasant odors, non-removable stains and attitudinal family members searching for the perfect dirty shirt. Armed with this knowledge, I have applied the NIKE slogan to my laundry responsibilities and I Just Do It. Nonetheless, we need an action plan or a blueprint to accomplish our desired outcome—clean clothes.

Leaving all your burdens in the basket of your heart will cause an overflow of frustration and/or an avoidance of the concerns. Categorize your situations. Break apart your matters and consider the most prevalent detrimental problems as your focal point and then allow God to show you what to do to prepare for His cleansing.

The Children

Regardless of your depth of knowledge concerning the madness associated with cleaning dirty clothes, you may have questioned how so much laundry is accumulated. I have pondered this myself on numerous occasions to no avail.

As you might imagine, my abundance of polluted clothing comes from my children. This is amazing to me because the majority of their waken hours are at school in one outfit. The one outfit usually consist of a single pair of jeans or sweat pants, one shirt or sweater and underclothes. I also provide paper napkins, paper towels and all the other paper items necessary to clean messes and reduce items for the laundry. There have been countless detailed discussions about the fact that clothes that are merely tried on do not go into the dirty clothes hamper, but should be folded or hung and placed back in the drawer or closet. Appropriate clothing usage has been modeled and demonstrated in front of an adolescent audience and mandated supervised practice time has been instituted. So then the question becomes, how do my children and yours, week after week, time after time, manage to generate hordes of clothes in the laundry basket and on the floor?

As a parent and an educator for nearly twenty-five years, I can agree with what most all parents of more than one child will attest; children are uniquely different. They operate within their own God-given style and have their own cleanliness quirks. For example, within the same household one child may adapt a military-like standard toward hygiene, while another child is comfortable with the sweat hog approach to cleanliness. One child's clothing might be highly organized—folded or hung and arranged by item and color. In contrast, another child might regularly house clothing on the floor, bed and chair and display dresser drawers that overflow with a variety of unmatched items.

Additionally, the way in which children view laundry can also be influenced by family routines. As the saying goes, "The apple doesn't fall too far from the tree." Hence, if the custodial parent usually has clothes on the floor or piled on the bed and the laundry is seldom washed; children often take on those traditions as the norm. While on the contrary, if the home is routinely cleaned and the clothes are laundered and placed in their proper location; children learn this as their method of operation.

However, in spite of the displayed system within the home,

sometimes adolescents will evade the established family standards and operate from their own dominant natural tendencies that mimic no one. As a consequence of this individuality, some children must receive continuous, specific training on how to keep the laundry loads to a minimum. Regrettably, my area of expertise does not reside in teaching one how to minimize dirty laundry as my own children happen to share the collective ability to create mounds of messes that require my consistent attention.

How did your baskets get so full? Are you irritated and blaming others for your overflow? Are you following the patterns of your past and operating just as your mother did? Do you know a better method, but are unwilling to expend the energy to change? Are you afraid to challenge the status quo and upset others? Are you stubborn and refuse to address your issues or make modifications because you want things your way? These are questions to honestly consider if you want to experience a genuine sustained transformation.

What Do You Believe?

In addition to these laundry habit truths, whether you recognize it or not, your interpretation of the laundry routines and cleaning processes is also framed by your predominant innate belief system. For instance, if you view most of your problems as temporary, challenges as conquerable and generally maintain the perspective that the glass is half full regardless of the situation; you operate within an optimistic framework. This view primarily yields reasonable concerns, restricted negativity and an overarching attitude of don't worry, be happy. The optimist reasons that happiness is a choice, things will get better given time and that most every cloud has a silver lining simply waiting to be discovered. This constructive outlook can help ease your tensions and provide you with some level of satisfaction during the most undesirable tasks, including laundry.

In contrast to this school of thought, if you generally ponder the bad things that could happen, focus on the negative aspects of life, believe your glass is half empty or look at a budding pink rose bush and see the thorns, it is highly probable that you are producing unnecessary stress with not only your laundry duties, but also with all responsibilities in your life. You likely spend your days focused on "if only" and your nights agonizing about things that you cannot change. You are undoubtedly tired, irritable or sad. You probably construe most every obligation as a monumental endeavor placed in your life to keep you from true happiness. Quite frankly, this mindset usually causes physical and emotional exhaustion which journeys toward a skewed view of even menial tasks.

You must consider your own foundational belief system and how you operate as a result of it. What are your basic tendencies? Do you follow family traditions? Do you complain, ignore or look for solutions to your issues? Who are you at the core that impacts you both negatively and positively?

Since you are reading this book, it is probable that you can equate with the laundry dilemma. You may be seeking methods to change some part of this routine job or at least improve your adverse attitude toward completing it and other tedious chores. Most likely, you have concluded that there has to be more to this task (and life) than you have gleaned. You are weary from spending so much time on this chore and being repeatedly irritated by what should be a miniscule portion of your life's activities. Somehow you know that God has something better for which you should focus your energies and more in store for you than your current unsatisfying situation. You know there is some part missing and you are seeking to find it. It is for you and others like you, that this book was written.

After examining this book and learning about the purification process we must endure to become clean children of God, you will gain a joyful appreciation for both physical and spiritual renewal. You will learn that the overflow of laundry truly represents the problematic expanses in your life that God alone can dissolve and wash away. I invite you to read the remaining pages with an open heart and seek God's message intended specifically for you. As you receive His message, I believe you will clearly discover what is now unseen.

Laundry Tips

I have provided this page for you to record the reflective thoughts, nudges, answers and questions the Holy Spirit will convey exclusively to you. Please consider the following questions:

What is overflowing in my life?

Who am I blaming for my predicaments?

_____

_____

_____

_____

_____

_____

_____

_____

_____

_____

_____

_____

_____

_____

_____

_____

_____

_____

_____

_____

_____

_____

_____

TWO

The Washing Machine

*But in fact God has placed the parts in the body, every
one of them, just as he wanted them to be.*
-1 Corinthians 12:18 (NIV)

Aclose investigation into the actual washing machine and its cleaning mechanisms provides insightful parallels to many of the essentials for this spiritual cleansing. To begin with, in order to operate the actual washing machine, it must be properly connected to a live electrical power source. Without the complete joining of the two, the motor housed deep inside the washing machine, cannot be utilized as intended or begin to approach its maximum potential. In fact, without the linking, the motor remains cold, unmoved and essentially useless for its anticipated purpose.

Even a partial fitting together is ineffective because although the machine may start, it will eventually stop, causing unnecessary pressure on the motor and eventual burn out. Without a full attachment to the power source, the washing machine may serve as an attractive appliance, storage box to hide unsightly items in its interior or flat surface to stack collectables; but it will not be utilized in the way in which it was created by its designer.

Are You Fully Connected?

By the same token, if you are not fully coupled with God as your foundation, you cannot receive His comprehensive authority to purge your heart and launch you into your destiny. Without this direct, open connection to God, there is no searching of the heart, deep-seated cleansing or imparted authority for change. Even though you may appear to be successful according to the world's standards, you will miss your ordained elevation of accomplishment without an intimate, committed relationship with God as your sustaining power source.

Church membership without discipleship is also not enough. It is the same as having the power cord on the washing machine partially inserted into the electrical outlet. Attending weekly service alone results in inadvertent power surges that cannot provide the constant, necessary force to fully clean and drive you into your purpose. While your exterior may disclose an occasional embellishment of His presence and offer the impression of a strong bond with God, there is usually concealed sin in the heart and untouched gifts lying dormant within your very being that simply cannot be resurrected with an occasional swell of power. The partial connection is exhausting and encourages you to escape your efforts to change because just as you begin to make positive steps forward, you find yourself continuing in the same sinful activities that you were before you began your quest for transformation. Thus, an all-inclusive cleansing requires a full continuous link, otherwise, you will remain inoperable for the completion of your intended purpose.

Are You Open to Receive?

For the washing machine to adequately sanitize the clothes, it has to have an outside water source to dispense clean water through the water supply hoses of the machine. The liquid stream can be controlled by turning the handles on the two valve lines that permit or exclude hot and cold water into the machine. The amount of hot or cold water, as well as the force of either, can also be controlled by turning the corresponding valve handles in the proper direction.

Equally, even though the Spirit of God resides and runs like a river through all His children; you regulate the flow. You control the current of the Holy Spirit because God does not force His presence or power on you. For example, when you are participating in desired sinful activities; you often shove the Spirit's prompting to stop your behavior away from your thoughts. You make excuses, rationalize your actions and even tell the Spirit He is wrong because you deserve to be happy. In essence, you shut your valve to cut off the flow of the Holy Spirit to satisfy your own fleshly desires.

At other times, particularly during Sunday service and seasons of despair, you not only welcome, but you beckon the Spirit of God with wide open valves. You concentrate on the words written

in songs, utter prayers and worship God with an expectation of His
Spirit to flow. For all intents and purposes, you adjust the control
valves to accommodate your own desires, rather than leaving them
completely open at all times to allow God's Spirit to flow as He wills.

You cannot become fully cleansed with half-blocked channels
or erratic fluctuations of the Holy Spirit moving through the valve
openings of your heart. You must uncover your portholes entirely for
the Spirit of God and welcome the smooth current or thrusts as God
ordains for your ample cleansing.

Will You Endure the Agitation?

In addition to the clean water current for refreshing, the
washing machine also stirs, circulates and spins the clothes to aide
in the sanitation process. Some of the newest top-load washing
machines have an impeller at the bottom of the wash basket that
allows large wash capacity and low water usage, while upheaving
and dousing the clothes for cleaning. Similarly, you can expect
unpredictable movements and pressure from the weight of your
issues when God is cleaning you.

The majority of top-load washing machines; however, have
a tall plastic-coated post located in the center of the tub that mixes
the clothes. The appropriately named agitator has spiral-like fins
protruding around its post to rouse the clothes. The agitator scrubs
the clothes clean with to and fro motions and unidirectional spinning
removes the excess water from the clothes. The various speeds for
these motions are programmed by the Laundry Doers' selected wash
cycle. Like this top-load machine, God's pre-determined purging
package will likely agitate you in some areas. You will want the
motions to stop and desire to retreat to your previous comfortable,
dirty state because it is easier. Do not stop God's sanitation
process. If you do, you are trading a lifetime of peace for flashes of
unsettlement.

Although front-load washing machines do not have a traditional center post; three to six oscillating plastic fins line the interior of the tub to serve as the agitators to clean the clothes. The front load machine, like the traditional top load machine, also uses unidirectional spinning to assist in the cleansing process.

Equivalent to the movement of the clothes when they are being cleaned, in all types of washing machines you can expect to be unsettled when God is cleansing you. In particular at the beginning of your wash cycle, His methods will plausibly upset or even anger you because He often galvanizes you with erratic motions for your ultimate advancement. In essence, God raises His expectations for your acceptable behavior and committed devotion. At other moments, you can expect the waves to seem too forceful and high to avoid drowning. There is seemingly trouble everywhere you turn and God is silent. Still yet, there are occasions when His movements will provide great excitement as you being to recognize the change in your position and arrangement toward a positive, peaceful place.

In all phases of cleansing, it is vitally important to remember that God is advocating for you. He knows when to move you slowly and when to exert Himself vigorously and obtrusively to remove your grime and push you into your destiny. As you allow the Spirit to flow, the experiential moments of disorder, disruption and disturbance will become less flagrant and instead begin to serve as reminders of the conflict between your own desires and God's will for your life. The Bible informs us that there is a perpetual war between our natural and spiritual desires so when we want to do good things; we instead, choose evil (Romans 7:23). With this in mind, past experiences that you have selectively forgotten and present behaviors that you are insistent to continue are likely to be challenged. You may be pressed to focus on buried childhood experiences, compelled to recall and forgive horrific violations, prompted to ask others to pardon your own transgressions or incited to cease your current immoral activities. Past and present issues must be upheaved to help you receive the in-depth cleansing you need from the inside out rather than merely perfecting the external display.

Will You Trust God's Adjustment Strategies?

Apart from your pre-existing or current situations, everyone can anticipate being upturned and inverted when they are being methodically cleansed. It is part of the process for producing maximum use and longevity of your gifts as you operate in your destiny. In the face of the discomfort, just as the spin cycle in the washing machine is unidirectional, there is only one way and no alternative methods for the scrubbing process. You must be cleaned by the Spirit of God to become fully prepared for your future.

Furthermore, all washing machines have many intricate parts that not only hold the appliance together, but also work systematically to monitor and control the machine functions. The internal maneuvers work to ensure proper operation. Among the various parts, the off-balance switch automatically shuts down the movements and stops the machine when the weight of the clothes in the tub is not equivalent on all sides. This safety mechanism is designed to decrease the pressure on the motor, allow the Laundry Doer the opportunity to readjust the materials and protect the life of the machine.

Fortunately, God knit you together and provided all the complex particulars of your body that allows you to function properly both physically and emotionally (Psalm 139:13). He implanted common characteristics within all humans and exclusive qualities that you need as an individual to sustain you for your predestined life tasks. Your tendencies, knowledge, talents and gifts were all ordained for your ultimate purpose. Thus, everything fits together and supplies the foundational support needed for your final vocation. There is no part of your being that is needless or that will be wasted. Everything you possess and have experienced serves as a rung on the ladder toward your life's calling. Although many of the situations may have left you scarred and perplexed, God will use them to help you succeed. Just the same, as children do not fully understand the necessity of rest gained with established bedtimes, God's methods and life's struggles are time and again mysterious until maturity in Christ is reached. You simply will not comprehend the significance of most events including victories, calamities and nameless moments or their shaping characteristics until long after they have occurred. You can be assured though, that nothing just happens (Psalm 139:16) and everything works together for your good to fulfill His purpose (Ephesians 1:10-12).

Similar to the off-balance apparatus in the washing machine, God also determines when your life is unstable and needs to be readjusted. He knows when you are devoting too much time and energy to an event, person, job or other portions of your life. He knows when you have been under Satan's attacks for an extended period of time and have grown weary. With all knowledge, He recognizes when to cut off pressures and provide rest. He knows when you have reached your limited and enough is enough for you.

Often times His rearrangement of your priorities comes in an unrecognized manner such as dismissal from a job, sickness, shattered relationships or tragedies. Other times He will ordain life events, offer relief through people, highlight nature or use His Word to shake you into awareness of your skewed priorities. Still other times, He will take you into isolation and provide a double portion of His grace to provide rest from your labors and the enemy's attacks.

In a nutshell, God will dispose of some pressures, allow you the opportunity to readjust your focus and preserve your life for His envisioned purpose. Your task is to stay steadily connected to Him, open your heart to receive the Spirit's flow, accept His tumult methods for your cleansing and receive His peace with gratefulness. He put you together, knows your innermost thoughts before you do and prepares you with everything you need from all your experiences to achieve your ordained purpose (Psalm 139:4).

Laundry Tips

I have provided this page for you to record the reflective thoughts, nudges, answers and questions the Holy Spirit will convey exclusively to you. Please consider the following questions:

Am I fully connected?

Is my life out of balance?

_____

_____

_____

_____

_____

_____

_____

_____

_____

_____

_____

_____

_____

_____

_____

_____

_____

_____

_____

_____

THREE

Laundry Collector #1:
Dress and Mess

*You see, at just the right time, when we were still powerless, Christ
died for the ungodly. Very rarely will anyone die for a righteous man,
though for a good man someone might possibly dare to die.
But God demonstrates his own love for us in this: While
we were still sinners, Christ died for us.*
—Romans 5:6-8 (NIV)

My youngest daughter is rarely dressed in her school clothes when I arrive home from work because she changes her outfits several times during my two hour absence. She is a girly-girl who loves clothes, especially those with extra frills and sparkles and she delights in changing her attire to match her playtime events. In one afternoon my daughter may wear her Sunday-best dress and my heels, her sister's tank top and running shorts, followed by leggings with a long sequined shirt and then eat dinner in her favorite large-striped, pink and green pajamas.

Although her high school-aged sister is present to supervise after school, my daughter usually has free reign in the back yard and throughout the house to indulge in her preferred activities and refreshments. Be that as it may, invariably the majority of her dress up clothes will confirm the gathering of various afternoon snacks and lively undertakings. It is also necessary to clarify that she has not taken her bath at this point, so the pajamas decorated with dinner residue and chocolate milk are merely the leisure ones that could never be considered the nightclothes she would wear to bed after her shower. Needless to say, her school clothes and most of the food/dirt-covered playtime outfits usually make the laundry room their final destination for the day.

What is Your Mess?

As I reflected on the ways in which my daughter dresses and stains her clothes before bath time, I was reminded of how God allows us to repeatedly mess on ourselves before He bathes and outfits us in His own exclusive design (Romans 5:6-8). Throughout our lives, He endures our bad decisions, fraudulent practices, indulgence in unhealthy habits and selfish mistakes that continually splatter us with filth. During these pride filled play times and self-induced quandaries, we often take on a host of questionable and adversarial characteristics that are not pleasing to God. Such features as arrogance, resentment, depression and the like; muddle our hearts, cause us to think, talk and act in opposition to God's desires for us and ultimately push us farther away from our Creator.

All the while, God tries to make us aware of His presence by either presenting subtle clues in a still small voice or providing clear indications like the confident elementary student frantically waving her hand, screaming, "ooh, ooh pick me." These nagging nudges in our conscience and blinking red danger signs before the cliffs are examples of God's desire to help us avoid messing on ourselves and blatant indications that our behaviors need to change.

Despite the fact that we often dismiss the warning signs and choose instead to fulfill our immediate fleshly desires; God continues to provide the light for our path on the road that leads to cleanliness (Psalm 119:105). If we are honest with ourselves; we will admit that we are well aware of the times that we have played with fire, experienced the burn and ignored the prompts from God to walk away from the flames.

Regardless of our rebellion, with all the smut surrounding us and in us; God steadily beckons each of us to Himself to make us clean. It does not matter to Him if there are faint signs of our secret sinful excursions, proudly flaunted displays of our confusion or no visible emblems of the disorder in our lives. Our omnipotent God, who searches our hearts (1 Chronicles 28:9), wants to take us from our current murky state and make us righteous before Him. Fortunately for us, God does not choose particular people with limited or certain types of dirt to make clean. His desire is that everyone be transformed into His likeness, notwithstanding the amount or kind of dirt present (2 Corinthians 3:18).

With this reality ever present, God does not exclude us if we have plain-sight mess on us. God loves and wants to embrace us even if we have a nasty attitude about everything, a negative judgment toward everyone and every situation, a lie for every story, a family of four with no husband and three different fathers, a drug addiction, a shopping obsession, proudly practice homosexuality or other gaudy dirt.

God also longs for those who parade only faint symbols of dirt in their lives. We primarily tell the truth, except when we must lie to protect ourselves. We do not gossip, except when it is necessary to set the record straight. We do not overindulge, except when we feel we deserve to be treated better. We do not fornicate, except when we need the release. Although this list of self-justified lewdness goes on and on, God continues to seek to win and clean the heart of every woman who displays these behaviors.

Still more, there are those of us who have concealed filth and God desires to mark us as His own. We have low self-esteem, watch pornography in the wee hours of the night, play church pretending to be righteous, do not trust anyone, steal from the job, cheat with every opportunity, covertly believe we are better than others and this list of secret unwholesomeness goes on and on too.

Whether the mess is clearly apparent, hidden behind a $1,500 suite or undetectable to mere man; everyone has some degree of grime (1 Timothy 5:24). Furthermore to be certain you are clear, if you read the brief lists above and thought, "I don't do any of those things, so I'm pretty clean," your own elitist belief IS your mess. You have adopted the attitude of the Pharisees; "I'm glad I'm not like those sinners" (Luke 18:11) and put yourself in the Jesus category- without sin (1 Peter 2:22).

The Bible teaches us that we were all born into sin and shaped by immorality (Romans 3:22-24) Sin is disobedience to God; doing anything contrary to His will. Because all of us have sinned and come short of God's desires for us (Romans 7: 17-19); all of us have some degree of mess on us! Just like my daughter, we dibble and dabble in play clothes (unhealthy relationships and risky decisions), get dirty, wipe off and then switch to another outfit (dangerous environments) to get dirty all over again.

Clean My Mess

Thankfully, God is merciful enough to draw us to Himself with all our widespread sin stains rather than waiting on us to become what we believe is uncontaminated. Paul reminds us that while we were still sinners; Christ died for us (Romans 5:8). Although we are clothed in our dirt, trading one blemish for another; Christ loves and is eager to change us. God voluntarily takes us, even in our filthy state, through the necessary cycles to dress us in clean garments. He changes our hearts' desires away from sinful acts to righteous deeds. We simply have to ask Him to do it and be open to His cleansing techniques. Accordingly, He will often have to drench and scrub us many times; but He will wash us white as snow if we are willing to let Him. Romans 5:20 says, "But where sin increased, grace increased all the more." Thus, God forgives us and repeats the process of cleaning us as we persistently get messy. Much like the dirty laundry never ceases, our own uncontrolled sin never stops, so He lovingly continues refreshing us. Although we should mature and avoid some sins; God has to constantly cleanse us because we reside in a sin fallen world and constantly trudge through smudge (Isaiah 13:11).

As our grunge is being washed away, God then begins to clothe us in His righteousness. He changes our attitude about ourselves and others, teaches us how to tell the truth, rids us of addictions, shows us how to accept and give love, helps us avoid becoming prideful, clears our confused minds, opens our blinded eyes and brings us into an intimate relationship with Him. He gives us a garment of praise for our despair and a crown of beauty for our ashes (Isaiah 61:3).

If God is currently applying pressure to rid the filth and extreme pain is being inflicted, you must be thankful, for He is cleansing you. He is scouring away the flagrant evidence of your past mistakes. Although this cleansing is not pleasant, it is comforting to know that God disciplines those He loves (Proverbs 3:12). He has a goal of making us better people, more like Jesus Christ. Furthermore, joy comes in realizing that over time with a good scrub and rinse; some relationships are restored and we can become clean.

Permanent Stains

It is also important to remain encouraged if you see slight indicators of your past sins even after God cleanses you. Just like my daughter's clothing sometimes becomes stained from her excursions, some of your chaos leaves evidence that simply will not fade. For instance, if my daughter has eaten food with a strong tomato base and it is not cleaned immediately, the clothing will retain a faint yellow discoloring for the duration of its usage. Similarly, if you have been messing up for a long time and have not tried to change, some signs of your past disorder may still be apparent even after God cleanses you. You may still have a tainted reputation, broken connections or lost friendships as there are some relationships that simply will not be repaired or scrubbed beyond evidence. Some confirmations of past sins will not disappear.

Nevertheless, it is essential to realize that some stains, while not pleasant to the eyes, may be profitable to remain. They can be used as reminders of past sins that should never be repeated. In essence, these marks should be ever-present reminders for you to look back and learn, rather than to go back and experience.

Finally, you must recognize that your current fixation on your sin stains is only temporary. Just as my daughter outgrows her clothes, you too, will grow past some things and some people if you incessantly seek the cleansing of God. He will take you in your ungodly state and show His love for you. If you commit to reading His word, listening to Him, worshipping and thanking Him for His goodness, your focus will shift from where you have been to where He is leading you. You will witness the fading effervescence of the dirt and your former iniquities will become less important to you as God creates you anew, changing your heart and transforming your mind (2 Corinthians 3:17-18). Accordingly, you will grow to understand that there is no condemnation for those who are in Christ Jesus because He washes your messy sins away and demonstrates His boundless love for you (Romans 8:1-2).

Laundry Tips

I have provided this page for you to record the reflective thoughts, nudges, answers and questions the Holy Spirit will convey exclusively to you. Please consider the following questions:

What is my mess?

What/Who have I outgrown and need to remove from my life?

_____

_____

_____

_____

_____

_____

_____

_____

_____

_____

_____

_____

_____

_____

_____

_____

_____

Laundry Collector #2:
Costume Characters

For I know the plans I have for you declares the Lord, a plan to prosper
you and not to harm you, plans to give you hope and a future.
Then you will call upon me and come and pray to me, and I will listen to you.
You will seek me and find me when you seek me with all your heart.
-Jeremiah 29: 11-13 (NIV)

Comparable to my daughter, my son likes to dress in multiple costumes based on his favorite characters. He may wear Spiderman, John Cena, Bible Man or Pirates of the Caribbean outfits all in one afternoon. He says the Pirate costume makes him look like Jesus because of the long dreadlocks in the wig! Or he may be suited in his own clothes playing the role of a preacher, followed by a policeman, Superman, Thor or a Roman soldier. I suppose extraordinary powers fit the theme for that day.

His role playing has always been somewhat captivating and amusing to the many adults who have witnessed his character performances. They praise his adornments as his attire immediately seizes their attention. His enactments, regardless of the many flaws, are applauded and deemed marvelous in conjunction with the costumes.

Perfected Portrayals

It is interesting; however, that no one has ever publically compared his dramas to the repetitive depictions commonly played out by adults. For just as my son dresses as multiple characters on a given day and pretends he is someone other than himself, most adults also try on numerous outfits and intentionally role play throughout their lives.

Perhaps the adult role playing goes unnoticed due to the perfected portrayals and longevity of the character being impersonated. Conceivably, the adult has stayed in character so long that she, unbeknownst to even herself, has become the personality. In addition, the adult performances may also be disregarded because of the unspoken expectations naturally predicted by her social status and outward decorations. As a result, the audience does not see the performer at all, but what is anticipated of her behavior in light of her presumed self-assurance and position. With this shallow vision, many women routinely dress in character and maintain undetected academy award winning performances for nearly everyone in their environment.

Throughout our lives we purposefully adopt characteristics of our friends, neighbors, co-workers and others as they have qualities and abilities that we long to possess, but believe are absent in our makeup. These admirable acquaintances often speak with cute, catchy or defining phrases and have alluring behaviors that attract the attention of both males and females alike. They dress in the most contemporary fashions and model cutting-edge hair styles. Because we esteem these popular features; we often duplicate them as our own.

Although replicating positive traits from others can be a healthy sign of desired growth, like my son, we fail to braid these constructive qualities into the strands of our own true personality. Instead, we choose to dismiss our real identities and become the character we believe is more befitting for the season of our lives.

I Do Not Like Myself

Most of the time, we fluctuate between and switch roles because we are not content with who we are and secretly do not like ourselves. In fact, we often abhor our physical characteristics, dislike our personalities and are frustrated with our very existence. As a result, we pretend that we are some significant other as we seek to flawlessly display ourselves through the character we are currently portraying. To hide ourselves even more, we persuade our friends to further define us by our career, education or spouse within the role we are acting out. Consequently, we perform for our co-workers, fellow church members and even our family members as we suppress our actual identities to portray what we believe is a more acceptable, likeable person.

In these roles, we say what is believed to be the right words and dress in the appropriate attire, all the while feeling secretly sad and empty on the inside. We become chameleons fading into our environment so as to fit in. We hope no one will recognize the loneliness in our eyes, forced laughter from our throats or disguise blanketing our physique. We swallow our tears, suppress our frustrations, paste on a smile and slip into character for each new day to camouflage our genuine uncertain essence.

What Am I Worth?

We also dress in costume and hide from our true center because we have not acknowledged and embraced the fact that we are fearfully and wonderfully made by God (Psalm 139:14). We ultimately fail to recognize our own self-worth. We do not comprehend that God has specifically designed each of us as unique individuals with gifts and talents of our own (Romans 8:29-30). We have not grasped the fact that we are made in God's image (Genesis 1:27) or accepted that He knit us together in our mothers' wombs (Psalm 139:13). We simply do not understand that God is in control of all things and He does not make mistakes (Deuteronomy 32:4). He either arranges or allows everything to happen (Psalm 139:16).

Our failure to recognize our value may reside in the fact that we never felt truly accepted for who we are since our youth. Perhaps the references to our lack of intelligence, overeating, skinny body, dark skin, bright complexion or nappy hair became the catalyst for our need to become someone else. Plausibly, even as adults, these conversations continue to play full blast in our heads with the summation that we are not good enough to be accepted; therefore, we must take on another person's persona to become a worthy candidate for love.

Unfortunately in many cases, we have been so busy trying to be someone else that we have long forgotten or possibly never truly known who we are. Every thought and most of our actions are centered on a predetermined suitable character. We have role played for so long that we have murdered, cremated and in many cases preached the eulogy of the person God formed us to be.

It's God's Fault

As a replacement for studying and accepting our core being, we secretly blame God and are disappointed in Him for not making us like we think we should be. We are irritated with God for not making us good enough to obtain adequate standards set by society. He did not make us smart enough to finish college, innovative enough to own a business, intriguing enough to hold a crowd, wealthy enough to avoid financial struggle, attractive enough to be noticed or even thin enough to shop in regular stores. In our hearts, we believe and subsequently live as though God did a poor job of manufacturing us so, we must dress in costume to compensate for our defective assemblage. We cover up and disappear behind others, while refusing to believe that every design is perfect for what God has planned for each life.

We have to trust His construction of our being and His plan for our lives. After all, He alone, knows our future and exactly what we will need to excel through the next stages of our existence. He knows the depth needed for our foundation and the number of pillars necessary to firmly hold the weight of our destiny's end. Thus, He did not craft our neighbors, fellow choir members and friends with perfected features and then flaw the design for us. He did not forget to add our talents or fail to gift us. We are made just as God, the designer of the universe, all-powerful controller of all, predetermined us to be (Job 37:14-16).

The book of Ephesians (2:10) reminds us that, "We are God's workmanship, created in Christ Jesus to do good works, which God prepared in advance for us to do." In other words, we are God's masterpiece formed to do what He has planned for our individual lives. What right do we have to label God's work as inferior? Can the produced tell the producer He made some mistakes, calculated the wrong plan and botched the project? Who can form a more magnificent piece of art? How can we question the architect of the universe, maker of the sun, moon and stars, sustainer of world balance and designer of the intricate functions of the human body? How can we question He who knows all and is in all? The apostle Paul addressed this very issue in Romans 9:20-21 which says, "But who are you, O man to talk back to God? Shall what is formed say to him who formed it, 'Why did you make me like this?' Does not the potter have the right to make out of the same lump of clay some for noble purposes and some for common use?"

Is This My Plan?

You must ask yourself if you are struggling to make your goals a reality because you have a self-proclaimed faulty design and are absorbed in the plan you created. Are you viewing yourself as ill-equipped and substandard because you are interpreting the world through your own lenses, while seeking to fulfill someone else's plan? Are you fixated on becoming what your family or society expects of you? You must focus your eyes on God's plan for your life and seek His will to understand the roles for which you have already been equipped. Simply ask Him to show you His blueprint for your life.

Never Measure Up

Regrettably, we also miss our own lead performance because we spend too much of our time matching ourselves to other women. We compare our bodies to size four women, our voices to the Sunday's Best winners, our marriages to affectionate, conflict-avoiding newlywed couples and our lives to those rumored to have it all. We study these women. We observe what they wear, spy on how they are treated by others and envy their appearance and supposed prestige. We allow continual thoughts of their lives to parasitically infest our minds and control our thoughts. We want what we believe we see on them, ignoring the fact that outward adornment is fleeting and beauty comes from within (Proverbs 31:30). In her article, "The Comparison Trap" author Renee Swope adequately penned, we are comparing our insides with other's outsides and never measuring up. We fail to believe the Apostle Paul's declaration, "But in fact God has placed the parts in the body, every one of them, just as he wanted them to be (1 Corinthians 12:12).

More so, we fail to consider that the very sister we covet might be playing a role and pretending just like us. In fact, what we see may not be the real person at all. Therefore, we must carefully consider whether or not we truly want her role. It is best instead to recognize that just as our finger and tongue prints are unique to each of us, so is our destiny (1 Corinthians 15:37-39). Accordingly, our bodies, intellect and personalities were crafted distinctively for specific work that only we can do. We all have a place in this world and a purpose that no one else can fulfill or complete better than us. We cannot get out of costume and into our own character if we do not realize that God made individual roles for each of us. We cannot magnificently be what He did not design us to be regardless of the perfected attire and flawless performance.

What is My Role?

If you are discontent, blind to the fact that God created you special, or expend huge amounts of energy studying the roles of others, then you are probably missing what God has predetermined you to do. You might have a gift for hospitality, to teach, give or lead; but you will never realize your own gifts when you spend the majority of your time envying or inhabiting someone else's talent. You will not experience peace or find your place until you seek to change your mind-set and refuse to believe the infiltrated self-demeaning lies that keep you seeking others' roles. You must embrace the person God created you to be.

Paul's letter to the Romans (Romans 12:1-3) also reminds us to "not be conformed any longer to the pattern of this world, but be transformed by the renewing of your mind. Then we will be able to test and approve what God's will is—His good, pleasing and perfect will." You have to start with how and what you think and focus on what God has given you. You must concentrate on where He wants you to be and the roles He has designed that only you can adequately fill. You cannot live by what is expected of you based on your family name, spouse or education. Society's standard benchmarks are rarely aligned with God's plan. Stop living as if people around you determine your purpose. You can only be appropriately dressed when you completely surrender your will and let God take you into His ordained role and ultimate destiny.

It's Too Much to Handle

Regardless of the role my son is playing; I am guaranteed to find his school clothes, extra socks, shoes and at least one shirt on the floor begging me to relocate them to their proper place. You are probably wondering why I do not make him pick them up. Well, for those of us who have told our children to pick up their clothes at least seventy billion times; we understand that it is far less taxing to pick the clothes up ourselves. We do not have to be upset when the clothes are still on the floor two hours later; we do not have to shout; our blood pressure remains normal and we know the clothes are in their correct place. It is basically easier. I did not say it was best for the child; it is just relatively stress free for the parent.

In contrast, there have been a few times (not enough, I admit) when I let the clothes pile on the floor and then insist that my son clean his own mess. At this point, he usually becomes overwhelmed by the magnitude of the task and cries out to me or his sister for help because he believes it is too much for him to handle alone.

In the same way, when we play multiple roles that are not ours, we usually become overwhelmed and frustrated by the enormous energy it takes to maintain the disguise. We are overcome because with each role we take on extra baggage and feel guilty about the dirty laundry we leave behind. We pick up and discard bad impressions, broken hearts, anger, unfinished jobs and indescribable disorder, to mention but a few. As our chaos piles up; we become exasperated trying to fix the situation by ourselves and feel we cannot take any more stress. During this phase, we habitually run from the situation by shutting down emotionally, blaming others or physically leaving in our efforts to avoid the disarray. Somehow we seek an escape because we feel the pressure is too great to gain the desired order.

Often times when we are physically present, no other part of us is attached. We deploy robotic play performances repeating our required tasks without authentic emotion. This temporary escape from the chaos typically leaves us more vexed and short-tempered as we expect our acquaintances to interact with us as if they are productive citizens in or at least aware of our covert society. However, our associates usually do not behave appropriately within our secret world, nor do they have a clue that it even exist.

Instead of evading and sinking deeper into the pit of self-denial, it is at this moment that you must cry out to God for assistance with restoring order in your life. He is willing and ready to assist you. He will give you peace, power and a plan. His peace will keep you calm when traditionally you would have imploded or exploded emotionally and perhaps physically. His power will provide you with the strength to admit your hiding place and the ability to complete the tasks that you have quit too many times to remember. His plan will offer the road map and clarity on how to turn your bad situations into great opportunities. Equipped with these tools, God will show you how to get tranquility back in your life. Usually, He will not repair your situation for you. Unlike the cleaning of my son's messes because it is easier for me, God does what is best for us. He guides us through the cleansing process, all the while, teaching us how to trust Him and avoid similar situations in the future.

Useful Play Performances

Equally important, God will use your previous play performances to prepare you for the roles He prearranged for you. God fits everything together for your good including all the characters and circumstances you wished you could change from your past and present (Romans 8:28). He is able to turn every circumstance into a stepping stone for you to fulfill His eventual purpose for your life.

You must realize, the divorce was for the best because God taught you how to recognize and respect a Godly man. The job loss was for the best because it relieved stress and taught you that God does provide. The lost friendship was for the best because she was supporting your pity parties and helping you hold the strings that kept you bound. The affair was for the best because it taught you how to forgive and that God truly does pardon sins. The child's death was even for the best because he was relieved from suffering and you learned that God truly does heal shattered hearts.

Notwithstanding of the circumstances, roles or problems, God uses them all as catalysts toward your ultimate destiny. You may not see the good now, but if you wait long enough, God will reveal how He used your blunders, heart aches and other's wickedness for your victory. You must love Him and want to fulfill His purpose; while recognizing that He is not arranging events in your life to make you happy, but to prepare you for your final vocation. The Lord told Jeremiah, "Before I formed you in the womb, I knew you and before you were born I set you apart and appointed you as a prophet to the nations."(Jeremiah 1:5) Just as the Lord had a plan and a role for Jeremiah to play, He has an ordained starring role for your life as well.

Am I in the Correct Role?

Whatever character you are presently displaying, you must be confident that it is God's will for your life. If you are not certain you are dressed for the correct position, ask God to show you. God will let you know when you are playing the wrong person because despite your very best efforts, you simply will not fit. You will feel like you are a square peg trying to force yourself into a round hole. You will often think, why am I here and why am I doing this? You will consistently reason far beyond and differently than those in your presence. Likewise, if you are uncomfortable in your surroundings, constantly have to explain what you mean in the course of a conversation or exasperated from concealing how you truly feel; you are most likely outfitted in someone else's attire.

If you know you are dressed and playing an Academy Award-winning performance in the title role that is not yours, ask God how you can get out of the façade and into the purpose He has planned for you. If you sincerely seek His guidance and desire to be in the center of His will; He will show you the role for which you were created. He will give you visions, dreams and glimpses about events yet to come in your life. He will help you by opening pathways and closing doors that are not yours to enter.

Is your hesitation to change beset by fear of what others will think? Are you afraid to step off the shore? Does your real role mean you have to give up some things or someone? Do you fear being alone?

I am not suggesting you quit your job, divorce your husband or leave your friends. I am encouraging you to seek God and His purpose for your life. You must remember that Jehovah Roi, the Shepherd of all will guide you (Psalm 23:1); Jehovah Ezer will help you (Hebrews 13:6); Jehovah Shalom will give you peace (Judges 6:24); Jehovah Jireh will provide for you (Genesis 22:14) and El Elyon, the most-high, Sovereign God is in control of all things (Genesis 14: 18-20; Psalm 57:2). It is your decision as to whether or not you will continue to dress for play rehearsal, create upheaval in others' lives and leave dirty laundry along the way. You can continue to subdue the Holy Spirit and blame others for your unhappiness or you can be dressed for your God-ordained purpose and avoid the creation of a great deal of heart ache. The choice is yours.

You do not have to waste your energy regretting the past performances either. You can begin today by accepting God's vocation planned for you before you were even born. While no other characters will completely satisfy you; in the roles God has designed for you, you will find peace, joy, gratification and fulfillment. You only have to ask Him for clarification and direction toward YOUR destiny and be willing to submit your desires to His plans. He does want to give you hope and a better future.

Laundry Tips

I have provided this page for you to record the reflective thoughts, nudges, answers and questions the Holy Spirit will convey exclusively to you. Please consider the following questions:

Am I acting out an Academy Award-winning performance?

Am I a chameleon?

_____

_____

_____

_____

_____

_____

_____

_____

_____

_____

_____

_____

_____

_____

_____

_____

_____

_____

_____

_____

_____

FIVE

Laundry Collector #3:
Sanitize My World

Do not be deceived: God cannot be mocked.
A man reaps what he sows.
-Galatians 6:7 (NIV)

In addition to my youngest children's habits, my middle daughter selectively exhibits a borderline obsession with cleanliness. She sincerely believes if she washes her face, dries her hands or takes a shower, the used items along with anything they touch, collect trillions of germs and must join the pile of proclaimed dirty laundry on her bathroom floor. She further suggests that all clothing be thoroughly cleaned before re-entering her room to be utilized again.

This passion for freshness would be delightful if it applied to her brace-covered teeth, her bedroom or the garbage for which she is responsible for gathering throughout the house and disposing outside. Unfortunately, it does not.

I believe that part of her everything is dirty belief system likely stems from the fact that she rarely hangs any clothing on its rack. She leaves all used and unused fabrics on the counter, in the sink, on her bed or on the floor intermingling as if they are all dirty. Despite being told almost daily to put her things away in their designated area, she has yet to grasp the necessity of this concept. Needless to say, her poor habits result in most all of the touched items making their stay in the laundry room.

Because my daughter is so oddly concerned about cleanliness in particular areas, I am hopeful that someday her current grubbiness will improve to the extent that I will be able to walk through her bedroom without stepping on items that should be lodged elsewhere. In the meantime, I have concluded that while my daughter creates the mess herself, she expects others, namely me, to provide her with sanitized clothing and a germ-free environment in which to live.

Expectations

As I deliberated my daughter's poor clothing habits and unrealistic expectations, I realized that most all people operate this way in various areas of their lives. To some extent we all want, expect or believe we deserve something or someone, yet we do very little to obtain the goal. More often than not, we choose to wait, with great anticipation, for someone else or an unexplained phenomenon to occur and make our dreams a reality for us.

Our thoughts are perpetually consumed by the future and what we believe it should be, while our daily activities are not at all aligned with our impending expectations. Why do we long for a different and better life, but refuse to alter anything in our current state of affairs to affect the change? What makes us obsess over our desired outcomes, yet not work frantically toward attaining the results?

Unfortunately, a steady peep into our lives reveals that our behaviors are not only derogatory toward, but frequently compete against our preferred endings. For instance, we expect a promotion and increased pay at work, while we consistently arrive late, spend the entire day texting, checking Facebook and begin putting away our supplies twenty minutes before our shift ends. We expect to spend less money at the grocery store, yet we do not plan our meals in advance and never clip or download coupons. We long for a bigger home, claiming victory every Sunday to accommodate our family's proclaimed needs; yet we have not stopped shopping or saved any money. We see sales commercials throughout the week and rush out on Saturday morning to buy what we have convinced ourselves we must have because the price is so low. We reason that a girl can never have too many shoes or coordinating outfits; although we have crates of cold, smashed footwear and clothing tucked away in the back of the closet and in the basement. We expect our children to treat their siblings with kindness; while we regularly yell and argue with them, our spouse and the dog. We want our church services to advance; however, we remain professional pew occupants who do not offer any of our gifts or talents for the betterment of the church body. We want a closer relationship with God, but we do not read our Bibles, talk or listen to Him except during the designated hour on Sunday morning. We want a God-fearing, loving husband to find us;

but we only go to work, occasional Sunday service, Kroger, Publix and Wal-Mart. We do not talk to anyone, but slip in and out of our frequented stops unnoticed. We do not show ourselves approachable as to gain a friend and then we complain that we have no adults with which to converse or significant others in our life. We set goals for great outcomes, but operate as if there is only today's fulfillment and no future objectives in mind. As a result, a keen observer would be forced to wonder if the desired outcomes are authentic or if the identified longings are superficial statements that we truly believe in our hearts will never become a reality.

If we want to reach our goals, we have to be certain to complete the required work, take the time necessary to prepare for success and wait on our efforts to evolve. Inserting shortcuts or avoiding any of these steps will likely delay our anticipated results or butcher the project altogether, leaving us perplexed and wretched with frustrated lives and unfulfilled dreams.

Prepare for the Outcome

There should be evidence of action and visual progress toward our goals. If we want a promotion at work, we must be committed to achieving success and working with excellence in our current position. If we want a larger home, we must budget our income, avoid unnecessary shopping and save for the down payment. If we want a stronger relationship with God, we must dedicate the time to, not only attend worship service, but also study the Bible and listen and talk to Him daily. If we want a Christ-like man, we must ask God to send us who we need and remember that Godly, handsome and impeccable are not necessarily one and the same. God knows the heart of a man, his experiences, disposition, habits and preferences. He alone can send the perfect complimentary counterpart for us.

We cannot seed potatoes and expect to get apples any more

than we can harbor bitterness and receive a joy-filled life or plan idle time and produce great outcomes. Our harvest will only be a result of what we have planted. It is guaranteed that we will reap what we sow (Galatians 6:7). For this reason, if we want our desired goals to be realized, we must be certain that our current behaviors are not counterproductive to the outcome and that the seeds we are planting have the capacity to yield the crop we anticipate. We must prepare for our expected conclusion.

Do the Work

While we do very little to prepare to receive our goals, we have the audacity to expect God to create a great future for us. We set goals for Him and make plans for great things He is supposed to quickly make happen. In the meantime, we ignore, procrastinate and refuse to acknowledge the work required by us to obtain the objective. While all of our preparation for any mission is futile without God's anointing; we must do our part and prepare (Proverbs 19:2). We cannot expect lavish results with our impending plans and dreams and ignore our required copious efforts.

Albeit God could miraculously and has on occasion, delivered everything needed for completion of His goals; most often He does not. He demands that we do the labor-intensive work. God could have freed the Hebrew children from the hands of the Egyptians without Moses, Aaron or plagues of frogs, gnats, flies and locus, but He did not (Exodus 8:2-24; 10:12-15). He required the men to present the case and commanded the animals to the Pharaoh's palace. God could have made the walls of Jericho collapse instantaneously; but He required the Israelites to march around them for seven days and shout (Joshua 6:2-5; Hebrews 11:30). God could have removed the thorn from Paul's flesh, but He did not. He required Paul to endure the pain with His sufficient grace (2 Corinthians 12:9). God could have prevented Jesus from hanging on the cross, but Jesus was even required to endure the agony and die to save us (Matthew 26: 39-42). If God required His only son, the prophets, His chosen people and animals to labor toward His goals, who are we to think we should receive implausible miracles and boundless rewards without any toil?

God's ultimate control does not negate our responsibility to work toward achieving our victory. Instead, He prepares us with the necessary tools to labor toward our goals. God will guide, provide a path and open unique opportunities, but He does not do all the work. God may have given you a great idea for a book, complete with chapter titles and an outline, but you must pen the words. He will not do the necessary research or force you to take the time to line the thoughts on the page. God may have shown you how you could be used as a missionary in a country foreign to you. It is your responsibility to learn the language and study the principles of that nation. He will not plant you there and impart your brain with a new dialect and deep cultural understanding; you will have to study the linguistics and the country's dynamics to gain the knowledge needed to be successful. Although God opens and closes doors and provides divine connections to aid in your success, you must devote yourself to the required labor. He will support your efforts in miraculous ways and use you if you have completed your part by being well prepared and are willing to expend the energies.

It is certain; however, if you choose to avoid the hard work and wait on others to help you; you will witness someone else accomplish the goals you had set and spend your days thinking, "I could have done that." God will impregnate someone else with the visions He gave you. The difference in the outcome will be that the next person may have the courage to press forward through difficulties, work without protest and complete the goal that was once yours.

Time Required

In addition to our required focused labor, we must realize that most great feats require time. Despite the fact that we live in a society plagued by the desire for instant gratification, most of the work required for any colossal outcome takes elongated time. Even though we prefer on-the-spot results, we cannot graduate from college, save for our dream home or create a marriage union within a few years. In fact, we cannot landscape a yard, makeover a kitchen, potty train a child or even launder our dirty clothes without a devoted period for completion. Just the same, we cannot plant seeds today and expect to harvest the results next week. The seed germinates through various seasons before it blooms. Although unseen to the naked eye, growth is occurring and progress is being made towards the outcome.

Comparatively, our goals are only realized after many seasons of effort, most of which is unbeknownst to the general population. You may have to work late at night or early in the morning while others sleep. You may have to sacrifice material possessions, vacations and family gatherings along the way to realize your dreams. Lavish results and sometimes even nominal transfigurations require exertion that can rarely be obtained as in a microwave. You cannot set the timer for thirty seconds or even eleven minutes and receive finished results. If you do, you will ascertain lukewarm products and raw results. Vast outcomes most often demand molding, shaping and firing much like that of hand-crafted pottery. There will be mishaps and setbacks along the way, but dedicating time for completion will prove to be profitable.

Equally, God is not a genie. We simply do not rub His lamp or say a quick prayer and all is changed. He cannot be tricked into making our dreams a reality by our empty promises. He could operate without pause and create whatever He wills because He is El Elyon, sovereign (Genesis 14:18-20); but He usually does not. Our goals, desired outcomes, wishes and destiny require continuous labor from us. God uses the work time to not only train and prepare us, but also to help us learn to trust Him and appreciate the results as we realize that He alone provides what we need to reach our ultimate purpose.

The Bible says "Commit whatever you do to the Lord and your plan will succeed," (Proverbs 16:3). You must ask yourself if your plan is truly committed to God for His glory or if the outcome is for you. Are you waiting on God to bless you with a great product while you procrastinate in your efforts? Do you believe God for something until the plans are not unfolding the way you like? You must be certain you are focused and working on His plan rather than your own.

Apart from our desire to change our lives and advance, Colossians 3:23 says, "Whatever you do, work at it with all your heart, as working for the Lord, not for men." Accordingly, our motivation to complete our jobs well, contribute to society, develop our relationships and move forward should be foundationally supported by our desire to please the Lord.

Unlike my daughter, if you want a clean environment, you must commit the energies to obtain it. If you have a dream or goal, you must work toward it, with perseverance until it is realized. God will help you, but He most likely will not drop it in your lap, deposit it into your bank account or even force you to labor toward it. You must concentrate, do the work and wait on the finished product; otherwise, you will miss your opportunity to flourish and spend your last days telling stories about what you wished you would have done. You will only reap the harvest from what you have sown.

Laundry Tips

I have provided this page for you to record the reflective thoughts,
nudges, answers and questions the Holy Spirit will convey exclusively
to you. Please consider the following questions:

What am I expecting others to do for me that I should do for myself?

What work am I avoiding?

_____

_____

_____

_____

_____

_____

_____

_____

_____

_____

_____

_____

_____

_____

_____

_____

_____

_____

_____

_____

_____

_____

_____

Laundry Collector #4:
I'm Almost Clean

Cleanse me with hyssop, and I will be clean;
wash me, and I will be whiter than snow.
-Psalm 51:7 (NIV)

My firstborn daughter has an incessant practice of cleansing her body. More specifically, she loves to take baths. She crouches in the bathtub and runs the water over her hands for two to three minutes before she even attempts to push the plug down to fill the tub three-fourths full. She truly enjoys the bathing experience. She reclines in the bathtub every morning before breakfast, every afternoon following school and every night before going to bed.

I could appreciate this need to soak in water if she participated in any sports or had an overactive thyroid gland that caused mammoth perspiration. I could also try to understand if she had any physically exerting activities, but she has none. She is a typical teenager with predictable routine behaviors. She arrives home from school, turns on the flat screen, eats a microwaved snack, talks on her cell phone, takes a bath, views the latest Beyoncé YouTube videos, completes her homework, eats dinner, watches television, loads the dishwasher and takes a bath before going to bed. How is she getting so dirty?

After all, it is not as if she has to construct the television, cell phone or computer using old secondhand parts salvaged from a dumpster or land fill. She is not harvesting her food from the backyard garden or neighboring farm before eating. She is not completing her homework with a discarded quill and crushed walnut shells converted into bottled ink. In fact, with the exception of a few dust bunnies and fingerprints, she has relatively clean modern amenities within her arm's reach. Be that as it may, one would assume that a simple douse of hand sanitizer or washing of her hands with a squirt of liquid soap would clean most all the gathered waste attained from her activities. However, she chooses instead to take a lengthy bath. What could she possibly have gathered on her person that requires submersion in water multiple times per day?

Unquestionably with every bathtub experience, she uses freshly washed cloths and towels and changes her outfits; which must match to perfection, even the "I'm staying home for the rest of the evening" attire. As you would expect, her bathing supplies and coordinating fashions eventually make their way to the laundry room to be washed by the devoted Laundry Doer.

Expeditions

My daughter's ceaseless bathing habits provoked me to think about the paths many of us take on our frequent expeditions to become new and improved people. This journey is frequently housed in a New Year's resolution, pre-summer mission, office staff competition or inadvertent whim. Whatever the motivation, we are recurrently focused on upgrading areas within our lives we have judged as tainted. Most of the time, it is not the fleshly dirt that we pledge to sanitize, but rather the habits and idiosyncrasies that continuously urge us to disinfect ourselves. Somehow we know the routines and activities in which we participate are not best for us and are detrimental to both our body and soul. This uncomfortable state of conflict forces us to regularly make attempts to adjust our behaviors and modify our lifestyles.

Whether the goal has been to lose weight, stop cursing, refrain from sex outside of marriage or study the Bible; the voyage has likely been a struggle and without long-term or absolute success. Despite the repeated attempts and passionate determination to conquer, we usually find ourselves right back in the same position as before within a few months, days or sometimes even hours.

It's All About Me

Principally, there are a few overarching reasons why we are unsuccessful in our quests for improvements. Many of us feel we deserve pleasures and bonuses in life because we work so hard, sacrifice so much private time and have put our dreams on hold to support others. With this mindset, we are often sidetracked by the temptation of things we believe we are worthy of partaking or are certain we have earned. However, this narcissistic attitude is counterproductive to our positive progression and obstructs sustained success. For just as we begin to make strides toward enhancement, our voice of justification whispers, "It's your right, you've earned it; go ahead and indulge." Thus, the advancement toward becoming a better you is flung off course and set aside for another day.

The continual rationalization of our small habits and questionable actions escort us down the road to the unsettled, guilty feelings we experience later. We tell ourselves that one bite of cake will not blow the diet, but that bite turns into weekly and then daily sugar filled indulgences. We tell ourselves that we would not curse if it were not for the mishaps in the kitchen, others only knew how to drive or people did not pluck our very last nerve. We tell ourselves one hug will not hurt, but that embrace turns into an intimate bedroom experience. We even tell ourselves that quickly viewing Facebook, Twitter and Instagram post without responding will not take much time, but that connection to update us on what is happening in others' lives lasts until we completely forget about our intent to connect with God.

These short validating conversations with ourselves block our focus toward change and keep us striving to improve during our next rotation of attempts. As commendable as it is that we recognize the need to become better people, it is difficult to celebrate when we only make nominal progress and never reach the goal. We repeat the series of efforts to advance much like the cyclist on the stationary bike never going anywhere, but exhausted from the labor. These tiring efforts compete against our desire to change and support our return to the "I deserve" focus.

I Am Comfortable

Our lack of goal reaching success is further hampered by

our desire to be comfortable and maintain routine procedures. We basically do not like change. While usually dull, we like our lives to remain calm and business-as-usual because it is easier than navigating the uncertain. We know what and how things will generally happen. We can foretell our week's activities, work responsibilities and others' behaviors. We have mastered the procedures and can anticipate the next steps. We do not have to prepare, add any additional requirements or be anxious about the unexpected. In essence, despite our desire for change, we refuse to get out of our boat because we are convinced the water is deep, the wind is fierce and the journey to the other shore is unclear. Truthfully, we are not even sure there is a shore on the other side, so we remain safely devoted to our existing controlled environment while gazing at the horizon and longing for mysterious alterations in our lives.

More so, although we want our lives to be different, we do not want to experience the required actions for change as they are neither easy nor foreseeable. As a consequence, we find ourselves in a rut fossilized in our current state by fear of the unknown. We repetitively visit the same places, talk to the same people and participate in the same events. We have no dialogue nor associate with anyone outside our narrow circle of friends, as this is our place of comfort and we have concluded others are likely crazy anyway. We do not eat foods foreign to us; but rather claim we do not like what we have never allowed to touch our lips. We do not shop in a variety of stores; but maintain our loyalty to the same stores we have patronized for years despite their distant location, elevated prices and dated attire.

To change our behaviors and obtain a different outcome, we have to get off the observation deck and figure out another approach to move forward that confirms progress. We have to be willing to cast aside our fears and attempt endeavors we have never tried before, go places we have never gone and stretch ourselves in areas we have never considered expanding.

I Am in Control

We are not successful in our efforts to improve because we go with our own plan for change rather than of seeking God's guidance for the process. In fact, most of the time we deliberately attempt to make changes without God because we want to be in control and handle our own issues. We reason that God does not understand or even care about our mere mortal problems as they are microscopic in comparison to governing the universe. We ignore the fact that He lived on earth as Jesus (Hebrews 5:7) and is acquainted with grief (Isaiah 53:3). We limit His abilities to our finite minds and fail to believe that there is no space void of Him or dilemma with which He is not aware (Psalms 139:8 & 9). In reality, we have not grasped how wide, deep or long His love is for us (Ephesians 3:18). We do not understand that He is concerned about every facet of our lives. Thus, we try to clean ourselves without success for years. We attempt to live righteous and try scheme after scheme only to find that within days and sometimes minutes we harbor the stench of fallen and failed efforts.

Meanwhile, we also fail to recall that the Bible teaches us that when we would do good, evil is present (Romans 7:21) and the Spirit is willing, but the flesh is weak (Mark 14:38). Despite our best efforts, we cannot achieve sustained improvements on our own. Like repeated baths produce dirty laundry, continual failed efforts results in a downward spiral of sadness, depression and hopelessness. The lower we go, the harder it is to get up, so we eventually give up, believing we can never change. Consequently, we smoke more, plan more opportunities for intimacy, organize idle time, bake the goodies and start the gossip.

We must come to believe that regardless of the number of baths taken or concerted efforts; only God can truly clean us. Just as we cannot change people around us; we simply do not have the power to change ourselves. God's change process is focused on the heart which leads to both thought and behavioral changes (1 Samuel

10:8-10). As our minds begin to think more virtuous, our actions follow suit. God transforms our hearts so that we become more loving, gentle, patient and righteous. He gives us courage, strength and guidance on how to manage the troubled areas in our lives.

His guidance affords us the opportunity to make modifications in our lives without fear and angst because He is ultimately in control. Our portion in the change process is to have a desire and willingness to allow Him to change us. We do not have to work for a purified heart; we merely have to surrender our will and submit to God's plan for our adjustments. Even more, following God's strategy for our alterations takes us off the gerbil's wheel, changes us forward and yields lasting results that transports us closer to our destiny. God alone can sanitize and make us whiter than snow (Psalm 51:7).

Laundry Tips

I have provided this page for you to record the reflective thoughts, nudges, answers and questions the Holy Spirit will convey exclusively to you. Please consider the following questions:

What am I trying to remove from my life?

Why don't I trust God to clean me?

_____

_____

_____

_____

_____

_____

_____

_____

_____

_____

_____

_____

_____

_____

_____

_____

_____

_____

Laundry Collector #5:
Hidden Accessories

Trust in the Lord with all your heart and lean not on your own understanding;
In all your ways acknowledge Him and He shall direct your path.
Do not be wise in your own eyes; fear the Lord and shun evil.
-Proverbs 3:5-7 (NIV)

You are probably wondering how I, the Laundry Doer, contribute to the substantial amounts of laundry accumulated in my home. After all, as a working mother with far more children than the national average; you've likely assumed that at least two outfits are worn daily and consistent mishaps and multitudes of messes occur that require my cleaning expertise to prevent local authorities from condemning the premises. Your conclusions are accurate. Fortunately, my children have designated areas where most of the big accidents occur which makes the cleanup less troublesome and easier to quickly sanitize.

As for my clothing, with the exception of exercise attire, I can routinely wash several loads of laundry and only gather a small number of items that belong to me. Despite my hectic work schedule and the demanding parental requirements to maintain cleanliness and order, I do not create masses of dirty items.

I would like to ascribe my marginal laundry contribution to high level efficiency and superb organizational skills; however, these accolades would be sorely inaccurate. I was basically taught from a very early age how to minimize articles to be laundered. As one of seven children growing up in a very modest single family dwelling, my training revolved around recycling most everything.

I was taught to use a towel more than once, wear blue jeans twice before laundering and hand wash the dishes multiple times throughout the day using one dish cloth (my sisters and I were the portable dishwashers). For years I believed every household operated in this same manner. To this end, I am merely conditioned not to place every item I use or see exiled from its proper dwelling into the laundry basket.

However, in all fairness to my children, most of my daytime attire does require more advanced cleaning than most clothes. While the ladies at the dry cleaning establishment know me by name; it is not because I frequent the dwelling daily. Thus, the ingrained practice of reprocessing clothing is extended to most all my apparel. More important to note is the fact that although my clothes are often made of a better quality than my children's' clothing and create a refined appearance, they require specialized cleaning to preserve their useful purpose. They are not simply wash and wear or wrinkle free, but necessitate specific procedures to be sanitized.

The Perfected Professional

As I contemplated my own laundry collection and what it truly signifies in the lives of so many, I uncovered a predominant theme of what presents itself as perfected professionalism—perfected dress, perfected behavior and perfected expectations. These merits are typically appreciated as they are often distinguished by stylish and proper appearance, polished speech and consistent proficiency.

The perfected professional is well prepared, far in advance, for most all occasions. On the very rare occurrence that she is caught in an unanticipated circumstance; she quickly devises a course of action, changes the environment to match her mastered skills or remains quiet as if she is somewhat bored and allows others to mount the stage for the moment. This professional does not project the slightest hint that she is not prepared or caught off guard. She does not appear to lack anything or to truly need anyone.

You will seldom witness this type of professional dressed casually, without make-up or even simply relaxing. Regardless of the situation, she radiates perfectionism that is often coveted. She regularly receives comments such as, "I don't know how you do it all," and "I wished I was superwoman like you." She is microscopically inspected and mimicked by many others as the standard for being the exemplary woman.

When the professional is in her work place, she is quite frequently held in high esteem and envied by other aspiring leaders in her midst. She is noticed by her superiors and customarily becomes the undercover High-Flyer trainee for the next company promotion.

At formal events, this perfected woman often captivates the audience with her appearance and grace. She is even noticed and studied in casual settings. She is the lady at the soccer game with flawless make-up, spotless gym shoes and exact matching outfit who remains well-kept despite the drizzle. This professional woman is also spotted at the mall and grocery store, wearing what most consider Tuesday-meeting-day apparel, complete with three-inch heels. She intentionally plans for her activities and regardless of the venue, appears to have it all—poise, position and power.

In stark contrast however, while taking on the perfected professional's attributes can provide an adornment of accolades, rocket ship career advancements and star struck social achievement; the recipient must be fully aware of the undetected accessories that often affixed to wearing this envied label. The perfected professional is most often collecting an array of behaviors and attitudes that are contrary to God's will which leads her to believe she is self-sufficient and in control of her destiny. She views her time and relationships as invaluable and only pertinent for colleagues who can assist with her advancement. Without consideration of her actions towards others, she develops a drive to present herself and perform flawlessly in all her endeavors. She is independently pride filled and clueless to the fact that she has drifted away from her previous Biblical teachings and in need of a heart renovation.

As the Laundry Doer does not visually produce mounds of dirty clothes for the laundry room; unbeknownst to most people, there are heaps of clothes collecting filth that must be cleaned by more advanced means. Just the same, the perfected professional is acquiring deep seated attributes that impact her core beliefs and subsequent behaviors. Yet more, while the laundry collectors can make subtle adjustments of their activities to experience positive change, the Laundry Doer may need to submit to reconstruction of her foundational principles for major behavioral modifications to occur. This transformation is especially difficult because by society standards, she is an amazing, envied superstar who needs no alterations.

Who Deserves My Time?

As she is elevated to and makes her stay on a pedestal, the secret gathering of opinions, motivations and character traits are being established. These mannerisms sneak up on her as she begins to spend less time with her family and friends, but chooses instead to predominately concentrate her energies on her career and status. She devotes extended time to her work associates and important contacts, reasoning that she is building the foundation for her success and surrounding herself with the "right kind" of people. She neglects Bible study, ignores requests for volunteers to assist her community and compares her church service attendance to her work obligations to determine where she will devote her time on Sunday. She further convinces herself that she is behaving responsibly and others simply do not understand the way she thinks or what it takes to be successful. The perfected professional is certain that her actions are justified and her motivations are to secure her family's future. All the while, she does not recognize the defective internal alterations that are evolving ever so slowly.

Attitude Shift

In addition to the change in this professional's preferred company, there is usually a shift in her attitude toward her former close contacts. She concludes that they are no longer suitable companions because their conversations and activities are trivial and a waste of her valuable time. Further, she begins to view most of her previous acquaintances as dreary, unmotivated dead weight on her grueling quest to the top. She determines that they do not know how to act appropriately in the workplace or in social settings, so she avoids their company and defends her actions as efforts to make sure they are not uncomfortable. The perfected professional refuses to acknowledge that her former associates have become an embarrassment to her. Instead, she maintains that they are just "common folk" who have no desire to advance and will never understand her world even if she tried to explain it to them. She places little value on authentic relationships, but rather navigates through her contacts as needed for accomplishing her goals. The perfected professional develops a superior attitude toward the people with whom she used to eat lunch, discuss the latest fashions and share private family stories. She completely forgets that her former devotion to the Bible taught her to think of others as more highly than herself and to treat others as she wants them to treat her (Luke 6:31).

I Must be Perfect

Even more opposing to the perfected professional's previous convictions, she now harbors an intrinsic need to be perfect with every endeavor and live up to others expectations. She tells herself she must never be or even appear to be incapable, unable, unskilled, inexperienced or ignorant. She leaves no room for error or the appearance thereof. Instead, she believes she must always be able, efficient, excellent and expert. If there is any question regarding her abilities that could be construed as negative, she works tirelessly to prove otherwise. She will even create seemingly valid excuses or blame her subordinates for any incidence of imperfection.

As this professional walks in fear that she will fall from her pedestal and lose what she has worked so hard to achieve, her character becomes increasingly faulty with what she has determined are necessary white lies and negotiated values. She does not realize that what she once credited God for providing has shifted to assurance of her own self-sufficiency with rewards earned solely by her commitment to her career. She does not confess or even recall that every good and perfect gift comes from God (James 1:17).

Dethroned

Unfortunately, the perfected professional usually has to fall or be pushed from her pedestal before she recognizes how far she has sunk in her character. During her ascent to the top; it did not occur to her that as her success sky-rocketed, her true essence was being drowned. She did not realize the transformation in her casual conversations, compromised conduct or idolization of her own success. She crowned herself queen of the universe and declared everyone in her midst as her subjects. She dismissed all prods to check her questionable behavior. In its place, she deemed clues of impure acts as jealousy and assassination attempts spurred by haters who could never be as prosperous as she had become. Furthermore, although she relied heavily on her subordinates; this professional held that they were all disposable and not essential to her success. After all, she knew she could do all the work herself if necessary. She wholeheartedly believed she was wonder woman with super strength, speed and communication skills that could be grasped in a moment by her single concentrated efforts.

On the downward slope however, this professional begins to recognize that she has run away from most of her common friends and distanced herself from her family. She becomes aware of her supreme attitude. She believed she was superior to her previous groups, as their way of thinking and life focus was petty when compared to her significance. She also discovers that the people with whom she rubbed shoulders and committed her time are far removed from her valley with no intention to visit her there, let alone assist her in climbing out. The perfected professional is now isolated and believes she has no one to lean on and nowhere to turn.

The Need to Change

At this very low point in life, the professional can turn to God for companionship and assistance while changing her disposition. He alone can give her peace, teach her how to treat others with respect and reposition her focus.

To bring about positive personality changes, the perfected professional must first confess her errors, recognize her need to be cleansed and commit to spending time with God. It is essential that she consistently talk to Him, read His word, worship and listen to Him. To obtain her desired sustained growth; discipline, obedience and persistent concentration are necessities. This does not mean that she must be perfect, but the professional has to lean toward and allow God to wash away her smut and make her more like Jesus Christ. It is a waste of her time to converse with, complain to or seek guidance from others because her crave for change lies within her core and only God can refurbish the heart (Romans 8:26 & 27).

Fortunately, with devotion to God, the Holy Spirit will nudge the professional toward righteousness and she will respond in agreement (Romans 15:13). She will not only start to identify, but also amend her areas of compromise. She will begin to re-examine her motivations for achievement, consider others in her decisions and assess her time commitments. In addition, the perfected professional will learn to identify the individuals who truly love her compared to those who were along for the ride to the top. She will recognize the need to show respect and compassion for others, rebuild friendships and value her remaining relationships. The professional will recall that her Bible taught her years ago to love her neighbors as herself (Matthew 19:19) and to avoid judging others (Matthew 7:1). She will also be reminded that her success is obtainable only by God granted grace. This professional's descent from the top and commitment to God will further clarify her need to rely on God and the importance of living for His approval alone. As she remembers the first command to love the Lord with all her heart, soul, strength and mind

(Matthew 22:37); she will no longer seek approval from people. She will begin to recognize her ultimate goal must be to please God. Her faulty view of self-sufficiency will be converted to the realization that God has ultimate control. She will begin to understand that true elevation comes when she humbles herself before God (1 Peter 5:5-7) and not when she promotes herself or allows others to persuade her into gaining status by any means necessary. Furthermore, she will recognize the value in trusting in the Lord with all her heart rather than leaning on her own understanding, so He can direct her path as she acknowledges Him (Proverbs 3:5). God will keep her steady for the journey, remove obstacles, reveal evil people and protect her if she seeks and trusts in His guidance. She will come to understand that God alone can rid her of the filth she has gathered.

Although she may not see the transformation immediately, there will be adjustments in her nature, altered desires toward good and peace that she cannot explain as she remains close to God. Just as the perfected professional's decline is usually subtle, God will likely rebuild her slowly into His likeness.

Concisely, the perfected professional will be cleaned from flawed philosophies and imparted with a new perspective. She will learn that if she has to lie, manipulate or treat others disrespectfully to gain a position; she will have to do the same or more ungodly acts to retain the success. It will become evident to her that God will elevate her as He deems necessary and teach her how to master the prominent environmental forces as a committed child of God. She will be assured that if God promotes her; she will not need to fear removal as long as she is submissive to His guidance. God will transform her mind to seek Him and her heart to shun evil as she places her trust in His power and walks in compliance to His will. The perfected professional will begin to accept that she cannot be wise in her own eyes, but must trust in God's cleansing power and rely solely on His perfect guidance for her life.

Laundry Tips

I have provided this page for you to record the reflective thoughts, nudges, answers and questions the Holy Spirit will convey exclusively to you. Please consider the following questions:

In what areas do I compromise to experience success?

What are my inner most beliefs that need to be washed away by God?

_____

_____

_____

_____

_____

_____

_____

_____

_____

_____

_____

_____

_____

_____

_____

_____

_____

_____

_____

_____

_____

EIGHT

The Cleansing

Although you wash yourself with soap and use an abundance of cleansing powder, the stain of your guilt is still before me, declares the Sovereign Lord.
-Jeremiah 2:22 (NIV)

Whether you have been dressing and messing, role-playing and camouflaged, expecting others to clean your clutter, excluding God from your sanitation process or hiding behind a Tahari or tailor-made suit accumulating ungodly traits, there are some fundamental steps you can follow to aide you in becoming an unsoiled, vibrant woman of God. These non-negotiable strides toward purity are equivalent to the preparatory measures used by most Laundry Doers when performing their routine laundry task. Unquestionably, the seasoned Laundry Doer is keenly aware that failure to implement particular procedures during the wash cycle will result in half-cleaned, discolored or even destroyed fabrics. Likewise, for the woman seeking to have her hindering, familiar ways genuinely expunged; no established step can be avoided for cleanliness and peace to be assuredly attained.

You Cannot Clean Yourself!

As a precursor to the washing process, it is vital that you grasp the indisputable fact that you cannot cleanse yourself. You do not have the proper cleaning agents, know the required soak time or comprehend the wash cycle length needed to purify your own heart. Despite your best efforts, even you are limited in your knowledge of how everything you have ever experienced has impacted you. Situations you faintly recall, coupled with events you have suppressed and your present state of being are all intertwined and network with one another to cultivate your current muddled heap. Although some sin events are blatant and in obvious need of cleansing, the thorough eradication process you need is impossible for you to outline without God's divine revelation.

Hence, if you truly desire the unnecessary weight of your past and present circumstances to be lifted and washed away, you have to be agreeable to exposure and the ways and means God has plotted to refine you. Do not assume His methods will be the same He has used with you in the past or even comparable to the techniques you have witnessed Him use with others. There is the possibility that your purging may come in a manner entirely foreign to you. After all, God weaved every fabric of your being and He alone knows the intricate details of each circumstance and pressures you have experienced (Psalms 139:15). He discerns where sin stains are hidden and how to unveil them for scrubbing. Accordingly, whether a result of your behaviors or the actions of others, your purification procedure will be a direct result of the filth in which you have wallowed or that which has been flung on you. The process may not be like anything you have experienced, pleasant or even quick, but it is necessary for you to become a pure child of God. Without a doubt, trust in God's sovereignty is a required prerequisite for accepting His cleansing system.

Gather Your Clothes!

The accomplished Laundry Doer recognizes the importance of traveling throughout the house and inspecting every room in open as well as hidden areas for hibernating dirty laundry. She has learned that failure to peruse her entire home results in missed items for cleansing, wasted cleaning supplies, additional laundry day duties and frustrated children seeking to wear the perfect dirty shirt.

The same notion holds true for those on the quest for purification. It is necessary to journey through the totality of your life and gather all the scattered pieces for your loads. This can best be accomplished by honestly acknowledging the details of your dirt. God already knows anyway, so who are you trying to deceive besides yourself? How much baggage do you have? How many monkeys are you carrying on your back? Do you have childhood pains and disappointments that you have suppressed? Do you silently suffer from depression, feel rejected, harbor hatred or live in condemnation from your previous decisions? Only God and you know what you have done, are holding on to or are currently doing that needs to be released. Furthermore, there are typically some hidden feelings and events of which you are not consciously aware. God will have to expose them to you before they can be fully cleaned. He will clarify the areas of your life that need your immediate, intentional focus and the fragments that must be disemboweled gradually for you to become His virtuous daughter.

As you take time with God to examine your mess, do not get discouraged by the type or amount of grime that is revealed. God wants to draw you close to Him, sanitize you and give you peace. It does not matter what you have done in your past or are currently doing; God wants you as His own. He knows that you are not and never will be perfect on this earth; but He still wants and can use you for His glory just as He has used other women with complicated situations.

For instance, God used Sarah despite her propensity to doubt His power (Genesis 18:12); Abigail, even though she was married to a wicked man (I Samuel 25:25); and Tamar, notwithstanding the fact that she was raped by her brother (2 Samuel 13:14). He also used Esther, although she was an orphan (Esther 2:7); Naomi and Ruth as widows (Ruth 1:3-5); Elizabeth, in her old age (Luke 1:7); and Mary, while still a teenager (Matthew 1:18). Additionally, God intentionally included a number of other unnamed women who were impoverished (Mark 12:43 & 44), adulterous (John 8:3-8), crippled (Luke 13:9-11), demonically possessed (Luke 8:2) and had bleeding disorders (Mark 5:25-30). Despite their sins, conditions and limitations, God upheld each of these women just as He wants to make use of you, with all of your issues. He wants to take your mess and turn it into a message to help other women just like you.

Sort Your Mess!

After you have identified and collected your murky events,

it is necessary to sort your loads. The trained Laundry Doer will read the labels on similar feeling materials such as satin and silk to determine the appropriate cleaning method. She knows that washing contrasting colors and varied fabric types together can cause colors to transfer, shrinkage of clothes, tattering or even complete ruin of particular articles. She also knows that although the clothes have been washed and smell fresh, deficiencies in the clothing remain or have become grander.

Similarly, when you force all your issues into one load, your problems often become cross contaminated and confused, resulting in a seemingly worse condition than you had before you opened yourself to cleaning. The feeling of defeat is produced as you become overwhelmed by the sheer number and magnitude of your issues because you think it is too much for you to clean. Your conclusion, in reality, is correct. The enormities of your problems are beyond your capacity to fix, but they are mere adjustments, tweaks or a glance for the all-powerful God! You have to define the fabric of your issues.

To avoid the smokescreen and receive an authentic cleansing, you will have to analyze each of your problems close enough to determine their genesis. While the situations may appear on the surface to be identical; their origins could come from different sources. Thus, you must determine if your current sufferings have grown from a single seed and germinated into a tree with multiple withering branches or if your issues have multiplied from various strongholds that now yield a widespread array of rotting vegetation. For example, does your lack of trust, promiscuity and anger all originate from childhood molestation? Are you depressed with a poor self-image because you were referred to as the, little big sister, as a child? Do you feel the need to control everything and everyone because you hated your mother's silence when her husband bullied her? Grouping your issues together will likely cause you to miss the root causes and be deceived into believing that you have conquered problem areas of your life until the matters sprout again.

More so, if you give up or simply go through the cycles half-heartedly to please others, you will not experience reliable change. Even though you have been spring-cleaned and project a momentary pleasant aroma; the ordeals remain in a more disguised design and will eventually reveal themselves again in a darker form. It is vital to seek God with an open heart for aid with sorting your loads.

What Size is Your Load?

After collecting and sorting your issues into piles, you will have to determine the size of each of your loads just as the Laundry Doer does when washing clothes. This period is necessary to determine the water level needed to sufficiently wash the materials. In particular, the size of your problems determines the degree of focus and time you need with God for His living water to flow through you. This flow helps you operate by the Spirit of God and not within your own fleshly desires.

If you have been broken and suffered disappointments for a long time or have very deep-seated problems, it is likely that you will need to spend prolonged, concentrated periods with God, as your load is large. This includes setting aside time for prayer, Bible study, praise, worship and listening to God's voice; while avoiding elongated periods with social media, television and other devices and people that distract you from Christ. To receive complete healing, you will need to replace your idle and recreational time with concerted efforts toward growing closer to God. It is essential to realize and accept that just as the origins of your situations grew over seasons; it often takes a committed period to dig up and replace harmful heart roots with progressive seeds.

Are you willing to be transformed or do you want to stay an acquaintance of Christ, just enough to get in heaven? The Bible reminds us to seek to have the mind of Christ Jesus (Romans 12:2). You can only receive the mind of Christ by studying His ways.

Blatantly stated, occasional visits will not suffice, but planned, intimate daily retreats with God are mandatory for the woman that desires to be cleansed from the inside out. The size of your load governs the proportional quantity of time you must commit.

Do You Need a Pre-soak or Pre-treatment?

To achieve acceptable cleansing, the veteran Laundry Doer knows to pre-treat and scrub stained clothing prior to washing. By the same token, some sins marks involve stages to be removed. Are your sins issues seemingly a part of you and have been deemed by family and friends as just the way you are? Have you been ignoring God and playing in and around sin for a long time? If you answered yes to either of these questions, you might need a pre-treatment from God. This process before the overall washing may seem as though God is applying pressure so intense that He is punishing you rather than cleansing you. Do not become discouraged as this phase is, while penetrating, characteristically short. God is preparing you for the actual purging so that when the Spirit flows the dirt is easily detached from you making you a clean woman of God.

What Water Temperature Do You Need?

A practiced Laundry Doer will also carefully consider the water temperature needed for her fabrics because she knows that using an incorrect temperature can impair her family's clothes. She is well aware that some materials require cold water temperature, while others call for hot or warm water to ensure the dirt is adequately lifted and shrinkage, fading and damage is avoided.

The Laundry Doer has learned that hot water is typically used when washing light colored fabrics, wash towels, bed linens and soiled items to effectively remove grime, microorganisms and dust mites. Additionally, she recognizes that dark and bright colored clothes are best cleansed in warm water so as to avoid color bleeding and irreversible damage of clothing; while cool water should be used for washing delicate fabrics.

In the same way God, the Master Cleaner, distinguishes the fabrics of your issues and responds with the necessary temperature to begin the cleansing process without damaging your threads. At times, He turns the heat up, highlights or magnifies the colossal danger lurking around you. These situations might include newly formed relationships, recently adapted behaviors, life-long friendships or deep rooted beliefs that are undetected by mere acquaintances. While on the surface you may appear to be jovial, light-hearted and not swayed by the ungodly influences, God examines the impact of these forces on your heart and their obstruction toward you becoming a clean woman. Hence, He pours His Spirit on the issues causing a painful disturbance with scalding affects to gain your immediate attention.

In other instances, He adjusts the temperature of His Spirit to make you uncomfortable enough to realize that your behavior is not harmonious with His plan for your life. He knows and is sensitive to your current predicament and the weightiness of your situations. Accordingly, rather than pouring hot water on your dark matters, He dispenses the warm flow of His Spirit so that you will not be overwhelmed by His method, but welcoming of His cleansing to obtain relief from the heaviness of your sins and gain peaceful refreshment.

Still at other times, the Spirit of God seems distant and cold with no interest in cleansing or even communicating with you at all. You typically experience these times of detachment because the volume of the world around you is turned up so loud that you miss the still voice of God attempting to assist you with your delicate problem. Your focus is not truly on God and living for Him, but on escaping the problems and satisfying your own desires. This lack of concentration causes the oversight and cold distance you sense. You are walking away from Him and shutting Him out of your life.

To hear God speak and feel the gentle flow of His Spirit, it is necessary to quiet yourself both physically and emotionally. You have to sit still, seek silence, intently pursue God and expectantly listen. God speaks continuously through circumstances, people and His wondrous creations. It is your task to respond to His chosen temperature setting, whether it is hot, warm or cold, with an open heart and mind to receive the purification you need.

Rinse Option?

Some marks can be laid away with marginal efforts. The water drifts over the tinges once; they dissolve and float away without a trace of evidence they ever existed. On the other hand; however, some blemishes require piercing pressure to be removed.

Parallel to the stains in clothing, some life circumstances are determined to remain in the forefront, decorated and in control. If you have lifelong, soiled or unwavering issues, your cleansing likely requires a pre-treatment, pre-soak and/or an additional specific cleaning technique. This leading preparatory step before the actual polishing from God conceivably necessitates a double rinse after the cleaning process to remove the excess residue.

For example, if you are holding on to some habits, things or people that God is working to remove from your life; a double rinse may be required. That is, extra effort and sacrifice from you will be necessary to sever the bond. These areas are supposed fragments of your very existence and people that you have come to believe hold your foundation firm and cannot be released. You may have developed soul ties with them, much like the bond of a husband and wife as they become one with physical intimacy. The connections are so strong that despite your best efforts to rid yourself of the bond, they remain intact. Thus, God calls for a double rinse; namely prayer and His power, to remove them from your life.

You must accept the fact that everyone does not have the

desire or the capacity to go into your destiny. Some people are only with you for a season to teach, grow and help prepare you for your future. God never intended these people to stay with you. In the same way, some habits have to be terminated and removed for you to become clean. There can be no lingering scum of past sins to contaminate the new garments or halt the purpose God has prepared for you. Jesus teaches us that we cannot put new wine in old wineskins or both will be ruined (Mark 2:22). You must invite the Spirit of God to wash away all excess loads that are holding you bound.

What is the Length and Speed of Your Cycle?

To determine the length of time and the speed for which the clothes should be washed, the Laundry Doer again considers the fabric type and amount of dirt on the materials. Attention to these details is necessary because the selected wash time controls the agitator motions and spin rotation. In other words, the upheaval of the clothes to loosen the dirt and the turning force of the spin cycle to extract the water from the tub are fixed as the Laundry Doer sets the machine wash time and speed in accordance with the materials being cleaned.

While the majority of fabrics require a normal setting that washes the garments slowly, some materials are delicate and require extra slow washing. Still other garments are dense or soiled and demand a heavy duty, fast cycle to become adequately sanitized.

Comparable to the practiced Laundry Doer, God without pause governs the speed and length of time needed for your cleansing. He elects the time according to your unique circumstances, scars and His predetermined plan for your life. He decides whether your situation requires His delicate hand to gently and slowly brush away your issues or if you need His strong hand for a hard, fast or correctional wash. Depending on His programmed setting, your level of agitation of your circumstances could range from seemingly unbearable to faint nudges or a combination thereof. The cleansing cycle could take minutes, days, months or even years. Your task is to receive God's lessons, while understanding that He is cleaning, stretching and growing you to become more like Him.

To help you accept and embrace God's approach; you have to consider your situations. Are your struggles a part of everyday life in this sin infested world that you have not learned to manage? Do you have substantial afflictions that need to be quickly fixed? Are you housing hidden emotional scars that God is bringing to the surface ever so slowly to wash clean? Reflection on your kind of problems, acknowledgement of God's sovereignty and gratitude for His unconditional love will provide peace of mind during His procedure and length of time for your cleansing. God alone can remove your guilt stains.

Laundry Tips

I have provided this page for you to record the reflective thoughts, nudges, answers and questions the Holy Spirit will convey exclusively to you. Please consider the following questions:

What is God raising to the surface to be cleaned?

Do I trust God's cleansing methods?

_____

_____

_____

_____

_____

_____

_____

_____

_____

_____

_____

_____

_____

_____

_____

_____

_____

NINE

Conclusion

I have told you these things, so that in me you may have peace.
In this world you will have trouble. But take heart!
I have overcome the world.
John 16:33 (NIV)

It is necessary to seek God's assistance with accepting His perfect cleansing methods as well as gathering and sorting your issues. If you shut down the Spirit's purging and do not receive His refreshing methods; you will not bask in peace, but experience short snippets of scheduled harmonious moments that never fully produce sustained tranquility. The concealed dirt of your problematic situations and blemished tendencies will continue to journey to the surface of your life, upheaving your surroundings and ending your harmony.

To this end, to become a content, upright woman of God, you must ask Him to help you discern the true meaning of your laundry collection and open your heart to receive His directions. It is essential that you accept that you cannot clean yourself. You do not have to add another work responsibility to your schedule. God does not need your help to renovate you; but your complete willingness to allow Him to do His work.

As you read and acquainted yourself with the themes presented in this book, it is my prayer that you have grown both spiritually and productively. I trust that God has already exposed what the laundry collection process truly represents in your life and provided you with insights as to how you might need to be changed. I am further convinced that God has begun to show you how He moves through cycles and soakings to purify you. With every mud puddle experience, whether you willingly walked through it, stepped in it accidently or were pushed down in it; God wants to lovingly pick you up and wash your garments spotless again.

My longing for you is that God has disclosed how He continuously speaks, works on your behalf and desires to have you as His righteous daughter. It is your commitment to quietness that allows you to hear His voice and your open heart that permits God to make you unsoiled. It is hoped that in this time void of noise, you will take a new perspective on laundry and other unpleasant tasks. Expectantly, this growth will be so immense that it surprises you and others that you can find joy in completing all repetitive, mundane laundry like duties.

As your faith grows to believe in God's sovereignty, I pray that you recognize what a privilege it is to be the Laundry Doer because we have the unique opportunity to clearly relate our task to this small facet of God's character. It is exciting to know that God uses even our most unpleasant responsibilities to reveal Himself. I am confident that God loves the Laundry Doers and wants to keep us peaceful and growing through our laundry.

Laundry Tips

I have provided this page for you to record the reflective thoughts, nudges, answers and questions the Holy Spirit will convey exclusively to you. Please consider the following questions:

What does my laundry represent?

What can I do today to begin my cleansing process?